THE GENTALIST

Abhijit Naskar is the twenty-first century Neuroscientist whose contributions in Cognitive and Behavioral Neuroscience have helped the world tackle the issues of systemic racism, prejudice, hate, extremism, discrimination and biases more effectively. As an untiring advocate of mental health and universal acceptance, he became a beloved best-selling author all over the world with his very first book "The Art of Neuroscience in Everything". With his pioneering ventures into the Neuropsychology of beliefs and biases, he has hugely contributed in the eradication of religious and cultural differences in our world, for which he is popularly hailed as the humanitarian scientist, who takes the human civilization in the path of sweet general harmony.

The Gentalist

There's No Social Work,
Only Family Work

ABHIJIT NASKAR

The Gentalist: There's No Social Work, Only Family Work

Copyright © 2022 Abhijit Naskar

This is a work of non-fiction

An Amazon Publishing Company, 1st Edition, 2022

Printed in the United States of America

ISBN: 9798432721938

Also by Abhijit Naskar

The Art of Neuroscience in Everything
Your Own Neuron: A Tour of Your Psychic Brain
The God Parasite: Revelation of Neuroscience
The Spirituality Engine
Love Sutra: The Neuroscientific Manual of Love
Homo: A Brief History of Consciousness
Neurosutra: The Abhijit Naskar Collection
Autobiography of God: Biopsy of A Cognitive Reality
Biopsy of Religions: Neuroanalysis towards Universal
Tolerance
Prescription: Treating India's Soul
What is Mind?
In Search of Divinity: Journey to The Kingdom of Conscience
Love, God & Neurons: Memoir of a scientist who found
himself by getting lost
The Islamophobic Civilization: Voyage of Acceptance
Neurons of Jesus: Mind of A Teacher, Spouse & Thinker
Neurons, Oxygen & Nanak
The Education Decree
Principia Humanitas
The Krishna Cancer
Rowdy Buddha: The First Sapiens
We Are All Black: A Treatise on Racism
The Bengal Tigress: A Treatise on Gender Equality
Either Civilized or Phobic: A Treatise on Homosexuality
Wise Mating: A Treatise on Monogamy
Illusion of Religion: A Treatise on Religious
Fundamentalism
The Film Testament
Human Making is Our Mission: A Treatise on Parenting
I Am The Thread: My Mission
7 Billion Gods: Humans Above All
Lord is My Sheep: Gospel of Human
Morality Absolute
A Push in Perception
Let The Poor Be Your God
Conscience over Nonsense
Saint of The Sapiens
Time to Save Medicine
Fabric of Humanity
Build Bridges not Walls: In the name of Americana
The Constitution of The United Peoples of Earth

Lives to Serve Before I Sleep
When Humans Unite: Making A World Without Borders
All For Acceptance
Monk Meets World
Mission Reality
Citizens of Peace: Beyond The Savagery of Sovereignty
Operation Justice: To Make A Society That Needs No Law
See No Gender
The Gospel of Technology
Every Generation Needs Caretakers: The Gospel of
Patriotism
Aşkanjali: The Sufi Sermon
Mad About Humans: World Maker's Almanac
Revolution Indomable
When Call The People: My World My Responsibility
No Foreigner Only Family
Hurricane Humans: Give me accountability, I'll give you
peace
Ain't Enough to Look Human
Servitude is Sanctitude
Time To End Democracy: The Meritocratic Manifesto
I Vicdansaadet Speaking: No Rest Till The World is Lifted
Boldly Comes Justice: Sentient not Silent
Good Scientist: When Science and Service Combine
Sleepless for Society
Neden Türk: The Gospel of Secularism
Martyr Meets World: To Solve The Hard Problem of
Inhumanity
The Shape of A Human: Our America Their America
When Veins Ignite: Either Integration or Degradation
Heart Force One: Need No Gun to Defend Society
Solo Standing on Guard: Life Before Law
Generation Corazon: Nationalism is Terrorism
Mucize Insan: When The World is Family
Hometown Human: To Live for Soil and Society
Girl Over God: The Novel (Abi Naskar Adventures Book 1)
Gente Mente Adelante: Prejudice Conquered is World
Conquered
Earthquakin' Egalitarian: I Die Everyday So Your Children
Can Live
Giants in Jeans: 100 Sonnets of United Earth
Vatican Virus: The Forbidden Fiction (Abi Naskar
Adventures Book 2)
Karadeniz Chronicle: The Novel (Abi Naskar Adventures

Book 3)
Şehit Sevda Society: Even in Death I Shall Live
Handcrafted Humanity: 100 Sonnets For A Blunderful
World
Mücadele Muhabbet: Gospel of An Unarmed Soldier
Making Britain Civilized: How to Gain Readmission to The
Human Race
Dervish Advaitam: Gospel of Sacred Feminines and Holy
Fathers
Honor He Wrote: 100 Sonnets For Humans Not Vegetables

DEDICATION

To my sisters and brothers in Ukraine
who stayed back.

CONTENTS

1. To Kill is No Revolution

Hasta la victoria siempre - thus spoke one of my predecessors. But I ain't him, and more importantly, I do not live in his time. What appeared to be the right thing for him is not necessarily the right thing for us. What appeared to be the right means of revolution for a person of his time is not necessarily the right means of revolution for a people of a different time.

For example, if we are to apply the methods of revolution from the past in this day and age, then even the January 6 insurrection would have to be deemed an act of righteous revolution. Time has changed, so should the face of revolution, so should the means and path of revolution.

I don't care about victory. For me the motto is, hasta la armonía siempre - hasta la igualdad siempre - hasta la vida siempre. This doesn't mean I am afraid to die for my conviction while defending humanity, but it does point to something rather fundamental - it means, I can no longer accept the loss of innocent lives for the fulfillment of my mission, for the achievement of victory.

The means is as important as the mission. It is this simple, there is no more place for violence in a civilized society - no more. So say it out loud, mi gente - yo soy humano, alegria mi camino - yo soy humana, sonrisa mi camisa. I am human, joy is my path – I am human, smile is my outfit.

Exceptionally rare circumstances aside, killing a tyrant doesn't end tyranny. Kill one, another will take its place. We must strip the tyrant of all powers, while keeping them alive - we must keep them alive to make them see what a world without tyranny and cruelty looks like.

A tyrant is defined by their cruelty to people, a reformer is defined by their kindness to the tyrant, after putting an end to their tyranny. To kill is not revolution, to preserve is. To fight inhumanity is imperative, but how you fight that is also important.

Justice is not given, justice is taken - sure - but in your efforts to take justice if you end up causing more injustice upon the innocent yourself, then you are better off with your life of injustice. We are to build a society free from injustice, not just pass the injustice faced by us on to someone else.

And such a society can never be formed with the spirit of vengeance. The line between justice and vengeance is so thin that often it is almost impossible to tell which is which.

We must not retaliate harm with harm, but we must not stand by watching as figurine while a harm is being committed either. We gotta put an end to the harm, not as an offended bully, but as a concerned parent - parent of society, caretaker of society - as the heart and head of society.

2.   We Are Not A Species

Healthy mind creates a healthy society. Mente sana crea sociedad sana.

And what is a healthy mind?

A healthy mind is one which has a healthy control over its ailments, not just the clinical ones, but also those that are not (yet) deemed clinical by medical science, such as prejudice, stereotypes, vengefulness and self-obsession.

(Self-obsession is considered clinical to some extent, but it is seen more as a personality type than an actual disease.)

World begins with the One - when the One is sane, when the One is sound, when the One is responsible, only then the World stays in the course of ascension and assimilation, instead of being distraught with descension and discrimination.

But one thing I must mention - things will never be perfect, no matter how much you try - the idea is not to build a perfectly humane world, but to be the cause behind the world's dropping inhumanities. Es muy simple – donde hay responsabilidad, hay humanidad. Where there is responsibility, there is humanity.

The trace amount of civilization that we do have today is the result of the responsible actions of those rare few who stood up to the inhumanities of their time. Likewise, for tomorrow's humankind to have actual significant civilization, today we must make way for it with our actions.

We are not just a species, we are also a cause - the cause of community - the cause of dignity - the cause of sensibility - the cause of life, light and sanity. And that cause requires active involvement of each and every individual who calls themselves human.

3.   Revolution is My Meditation

Losing oneself in prayer won't do, losing oneself in meditation won't do, if we must be lost, let us lose ourselves in resuscitating this dying world of ours with our sweat and blood. People think meditation will solve everything. And to some extent, even I thought this way when I was a teenager. But the fact of the matter is, it won't.

It's not bad mark you, but contrary to popular belief, it's not the key to all the problems of society.

We need ten percent meditation, ninety percent revolution. Better yet, we need a life where meditation is revolution, revolution is meditation. It is this simple. Make justice your meditation, make equity your meditation, make love your meditation, and you won't need any of the traditional meditation.

The greatest meditation is revolution for assimilation. La mayor meditación es la revolución para la asimilación. Justicia es mi meditación - igualdad es mi meditación - humanidad es mi meditación.

Society needs your active involvement, not your pretend involvement. I'll say it to you plainly. If you don't wanna get involved, that's perfectly fine, but don't pretend that you are doing great service to the world by praying and meditating isolated from the actual troubles of society.

Worse than non-involvement is pretend involvement. Either get involved or don't, there's no praying. Either serve or don't, there's no praying. Either lift or don't, there's no praying. Prayer as means of self-sustenance is okay, but it mustn't be glorified beyond that point.

4. **Light is Law**

Someone asked me the other day, whether I'll ever run for office? Here's my answer. I'll never indulge in political partisanism in any form whatsoever, but the day is not far, when the entire world will be led by my soldiers, in politics, in science, in medicine, in religion, in every single walk of life.

And my soldiers are not to crave for solitude and serenity, they are not to sit in a cave and meditate for eternity seeking enlightenment, they are to rise, fall, learn and burn in bringing smiles on teary faces.

I say again.

Awake, Arise, break yourself, and lo your light pours as divine help.

Remember, you don't get light by seeking light, you get light by giving light. Light is a weird little thing, it defies all law of self-preservation and that cliché of survival of the fittest. You see, the more you try to hoard light, the more you lose it, and the more you share it, the more you have it.

Light has a law of its own, light is law on its own. It is the law of giving, it is the law of sharing. You may have heard of the saying, live and let live. My word to you is, the only way to live is to help another live – ayuda a la gente es vivir. Live my friend, live as the whole of humanity, as the help and height of humanity.

5.   Law of Light (The Sonnet)

Law of Light
(The Sonnet)

Light shared is light amplified,
Light hoarded is light lost.
Life is light when lived for others,
Darkness when lost in snobbish cause.
We are truly knowledgeable,
When our knowledge annuls animosity.
We truly have existence solely when,
We exist to elevate all of humanity.
Elevation of humanity happens,
One neighborhood at a time.
Time and space have meaning,
Only when they help our spirits align.
In short, there is neither time nor space.
Either everything is love or sheer nonsense.

6. No Time, No Space
(The Sonnet)

No Time, No Space
(The Sonnet)

There is no time, no space,
There is only love.
There is no intellect, no philosophy,
There is only love.
There is no defeat, no victory,
There is only love.
There is no loss, no gain,
There is only love.
There is no path, no pedestrian,
There is only love.
There is no mission, no means,
There is only love.
All of us are either echoes of love beyond chains,
Or just some traditional trash of glory and gain.

7. We Are Saint, We Are Devil

As long as you are thinking in terms of an ist, you are not living as a human. You wonder, how can you move past the isms - what is the way - what is the answer!

I say, there is an answer, you are the answer - tu eres la respuesta. Sectarianism kills people, racial profiling kills people, nationalism kills people, religious supremacy kills people, cultural exclusivity kills people, history has shown that again and again and again.

Our ancestors were idiots, most of them anyway. At every little inconvenience they burst out in violence. You are not them, you are better, braver, wiser. Then why do you have to suffer the same consequences as our ancestors did! They didn't know better, but you do - don't you! So, stand up and act as such.

Somos el santo, somos el diablo. Tenemos que escribir nuestro propio destino.

We are the saint, we are the devil. Our destiny is born of our own mortal will.

But mark you, do not confuse will with whim, though at the moment they may feel the same. The difference is that whim fades, but genuine human will doesn't. It may flicker occasionally, but it never fades.

If it fades, it ain't no will of a human, but merely whim of a barbarian.

So what are you?

It ain't a question of judgment, it's just a plain question of ascension. And only a human can ask themselves this question without being revolted at the mere possibility, that they might not be human after all.

8.   Humanity is Not Reality Yet

Only a human can admit they ain't truly human, while savages proclaim to be human absolute. Humanity is not a reality yet, but a mere possibility - a potent one, but still just a possibility nevertheless. And that possibility exists because of those humans who willingly acknowledge the primitivity within, while the others throw away all scope for growth by denying the very possibility of any follies in them.

And there is nothing uglier than the sight of a human boasting their inhumanity. Once you start glorifying your innate inhumanity, instead of correcting them, that is the first step down the road to degradation, and ultimately extinction.

The primitiveness in us doesn't need any coaxing to come into action, it is always ready to jump into each and every situation of human life. And a reckless human is the perfect vessel for such inhumanity, for they exude not a trace of desire for self-correction - all they do is self-aggrandize, which further fosters greed, bigotry and all sorts of detrimental disorders of the psyche.

Then eventually we have a society divided in two classes, the exploited and the exploiters, exactly like what we have today. And all this exploitation is sustained not by the exploiters' greed but by the indifference of the exploited. Indifference has become a fashion, that's why the bigoted morons can get away with all sorts of terrorist atrocities. But no more!

9.   What is A Reformer

Terrorists don't walk around carrying guns and grenades any more, except for the confederate nitwits and religious blockheads that is. Today's terrorists walk amongst us, perfectly indistinguishable, with a fancy outside and a filthy inside. And here's my word to these violators of human rights.

I'm a billionaire, I'm a politician, I'm a bureaucrat, I'm a diplomat - if you so much as dream of exploiting people thinking such filth, mark the words of this gentalist eternal - it'll take me two shakes of a lamb's tail to wipe you out from the fabric of time. But I won't. No matter what, I'll defend the people, and still spare your life. You know why?

Because, a terrorist is defined by how they treat the innocent, a reformist is defined by how they treat the terrorist.

So mend your ways my child, because if you are terror, I am your grandfather.

To take life is easy, but to give life is what makes one human. The point is, defeating a bunch of greedy people doesn't achieve much. To defeat the greedy is easy, to defeat greed, that's something. To defeat the enemy is easy, to defeat their hate, that's greatness. To defeat the animals is easy, to defeat animality, that's humanness.

And indeed that's what leads to a better society, otherwise, you only postpone the atrocity, that's all - you only postpone the inhumanity.

So I say again, the only lasting way out of this mess is to treat the environment. Restrain the peddlers of hate and inhumanity, sure, that's your duty, that's our duty, as human beings, but place way more attention on treating the environment that breeds such inhumanity in the first place.

10. Repudiation without Retaliation

More than anything else, we must place our attention on breaking the cycle of cruelty. And the only way to do that is by repudiation without retaliation - which means that we are not to keep quiet at the face of inhumanity, but we are not to cause further inhumanity either.

This may be extremely difficult in practical situation, but whether or not you are able to defeat this difficulty will determine whether or not you'll put in motion a paradigm of kindness over cruelty.

This is the prime reason, I do not retaliate hate with further hate at my haters. Someone must break the cycle of our traditional habit of cruelty. And if a conscientious human cannot do that, who will!

This has nothing to do with intellect, this has nothing to do with enlightenment and all that mystical nonsense. It's just common sense - common sense of a human being while being a human being.

You don't need me or anybody else to enlighten you in that direction, for that would imply that I am somehow superior to you. I ain't - nobody is superior to nobody. We are all messed up creatures trying to find our way through life.

So, let me make one thing absolutely clear. I'm not here to enlighten or awaken anybody. Anybody who says they can awaken you, is either lying or plain deluded. I'm just here to burn, and if you want, you can burn with me, for light united is world ignited.

Burn with me, not for me. Burn for those who have not a single helping hand in their life, burn for those in need, those in suffering, those in misery - that my friend, will be the rightful use of your light.

I am just a plain biologist, I can tell you certain facts about the biological underpinnings of your emotions, thoughts and behavior, but no mortal in the world has the power to enlighten you, except yourself. You are your own enlightenment. Know this, and you'll know the world.

11. No Superior No Inferior

You may seek for a companion in your journey, but never seek for a guide in your journey, for you are your own guide. Because if anybody else comes and guides your life, it won't be your life that you'd be living, but their life. For you to actually live your life, you must be your own guide.

But mark you, this doesn't mean you oughta foster a narcissistic mentality. It simply means, you oughta pledge your loyalty to no one, you oughta see no one as your superior, just like you oughta see no one as your inferior.

Religion, nation, culture or language, nothing must stand between you and the rest of humankind. And yes, this means cleansing your mind of all supremacist fondness for the so-called background that you are raised in. Let's take language for example.

There are those who eagerly learn another language to be one with another culture, then there are those morons who insist on the exclusive glorification of their so-called native language. The world is beautified by the former, whereas the latter only sustain disharmony - the latter only act as a prehistoric impediment to the unification of humankind.

So I repeat, be a fundamentalist of assimilation, not of language, faith, culture, or anything so prehistoric. In fact, in becoming one with people, even if you lose your language, along with every last trace of your so-called cultural background, that's not a loss, but an actual fulfillment of life. Because, there is nothing higher than unification, than assimilation, than oneness. In front of oneness language, faith, culture, all these are mere expendable trivialities.

12. Behavior is Background

To hell with language, to hell with faith, to hell with nationality, culture and ancestral identity. Enough I say, enough with this prehistoric primitivity! Unlike the savages, I am a civilized human of a civilized world, and my background lies in my conduct, not in some stoneage tribalism. Thus speaks a civilized human.

Make behavior your background, make behavior your culture, make behavior your identity, and the world will have all the uplift it needs. Remember - people first, then everything else. And I don't mean all that nonsense of "my people, your people", but all people.

But again, the intellectual idiots don't understand anything simple, unless it is presented in their savage ism-istic fashion. That's why I coined the term "gentalist" in my last work - to refer to the individuals with an insurmountable concern for people over isms - over all sorts of sectarianism.

To put it simply, a gentalist is just a plain human whose foremost priority is to be human, above all cultural, political, religious, intellectual and ideological barbarism. In fact, every gentalist is a human, but not every human is a gentalist.

But again, it's just another word. If you don't like it, forget it. Forget it along with all other terms and designations, and just be human. I am no intellectual, I don't care whether you use certain words coined by me - I am a human, and all I care about is whether you act as the human you have the potential to be.

I am a human first, scientist second, and poet last. What are you? You may have a lot of titles and designations in life, and that's perfectly fine. Just make sure that no title takes preference over your humanness, over your humanhood.

13. Beyond Politics (The Sonnet)

Beyond Politics
(The Sonnet)

Changing leadership, changing party,
These ain't change, but same old tribalism.
Changing the shape and name of tribalism,
Is not end of tribalism, but recurring tribalism.
If you really want to bring actual change,
Aim for a non-tribal society, one of nonsectarianism.
Replacing one sect with another may feel like change,
But it's just another form of unchanging divisionism.
Real change is when civic duty turns common sanity,
When there's no community service, only life and living.
The supreme policy is that of individual accountability,
True order comes through collectivity, not policing.
Stop relying on politicians for every little trouble.
And the world will be a place without political turmoil.

14. The World Sonnet

The World Sonnet

The world will never be a place without troubles,
But that is not the point, the point is something else.
The point is that most of the troubles we do have,
Are caused by our own archaic stupidity 'n shallowness.
Shallow and indifferent, that's the norm of the world.
With such norm how can we expect there to be equality!
Civilization comes from the ground, not the government.
The ones walking the ground are the cause of humanity.
Rhythm of the world comes from the rhythm of your heart,
Place your hand on your heart and listen across biases.
If there is music in you there'll be music in the world,
But if there's just noise within, all around there'll be travesty.
WORLD means We On Road of Love and Determination.
The aim is to conquer our last ounce of discrimination.

15. People Over Path
(The Sonnet)

People Over Path
(The Sonnet)

Celebrities defend vanity,
Intellectuals defend intellect,
Preachers defend scriptures,
Scientists defend factual evidence.
I found plenty of human professions,
But in none of them I found a human.
All are obsessed to defend their path,
Yet all paths are dead without a human.
No matter who we are or what we are,
Above all else our identity is humanness.
If this simple fact is still not clear enough,
All vanity, intellect, texts and science are baseless.
Before defending a puny path, let us take a human peek.
If we must defend, let us defend the helpless and weak.

16. Ain't No Sinner
(The Sonnet)

Ain't No Sinner

(The Sonnet)

When we think ourselves weak,
We become weak.
When we think ourselves sinner,
We become sinner most meek.
Yes we are fundamentally cruel and divisionistic,
Yes the evil in us is stronger than our good.
That's because our ancestors survived through cruelty,
They didn't have much scope to practice their good.
But we ain't our ancestors in our way of life,
We don't have to watch out for predators in every bush.
Then why do we still behave like predators ourselves,
Why don't we break this tribalistic tradition of ambush!
No more cruelty either on ourselves or on those around!
Embolden your backbone into a fountain of kinship unbound.

17. The Supreme Sickness

Everybody is worried about the population explosion on earth. But you know what - there is no explosion in human population, there's only explosion in selfishness, recklessness and indifference. If we could just overpower these primitive tenets, earth could sustain not seven billion, but seventy billion lives quite majestically.

To put it another way, overpopulation is not the problem, reckless self-centricity is. A society that has no grip over its selfishness, has to focus on population control. But the problem is that we've placed all our attention on artificial means of temporary progress instead of treating the root of all societal problems - human selfishness. Treat the disease, not the symptom - focus on selfishness control, more than you focus on population control.

It's not that selfishness is a disease (technically speaking), it's a natural, and so far the foundational element of the human psyche. But just because something is natural, doesn't make it civilized, particularly when we do have the brain capacity to replace such primitive foundation with civilization tenets like kindness, reason and self-regulation.

But again, don't assume that I'm advocating for expanding one's family beyond proportions, rather all I'm asking is that you shift your focus – nay, all I am asking is that we shift our focus, from symptom to sickness.

And the supreme sickness is selfishness (metaphorically speaking), not because it isn't natural, but because such "natural" ain't a human "natural". You see, earth has plenty resources to suffice our need, but no planet has enough resources to suffice our greed. And while we are on the subject, let me mention one more thing, since we've made such a mess of this planet already.

It's not that the planet can't heal itself, it can, but once it starts to heal itself, humankind will be eradicated as disease-causing germs. So whether the crisis is of climatological nature or societal nature, first and foremost, we gotta distinguish between need and greed.

A billion policy reforms will fall short to solve the ever increasing crises born of human greed, of plain ordinary selfishness. Selfishness is the enemy. And all peddlers of selfishness are my enemy.

18. Pray Less, Help More

Some may say, isn't it more humane to have no enemies! To which I say, you have to be dead to have no enemies.

And believe you me, I am not dead.

As such I have plenty enemies. Anyone who wastes more food than they share with those who are starving is my enemy - anyone who throws away more clothes than they give away to those without is my enemy - anyone who wastes more time in frivolous acts of enjoyment than they spend in helping those in need is my enemy - for they are the cause of all disparities in the world. I don't hate them, for I renounced hate long ago, but as a human it's my duty to bring them down to earth while lifting the fallen up to their rightful place under the sun.

And this ain't no ism, it's just a fundamental duty of one who's fundamentally human. But if you agree you ain't no human, I've got nothing to say to you. My ideas are for the brave of nerves and gentle of hearts. Because to the rest, they'll appear to be sheer stupidity anyway.

My ideas are for the accountable, my ideas are for the responsible, my ideas are for those real humans who do not brush off their responsibility towards the welfare of others - my ideas are for those who actually reach out to help instead of pretending to help out by uttering baseless nonsense like "my prayers are with you".

Pray less, help more, my friend. The world has plenty people to sit and pray, but very few to actually stand and help. And remember, there's not one, but many ways to help. Just choose any tangible means and help out.

19. I Am Ukraine
   (The Sonnet)

I Am Ukraine
(The Sonnet)

Peace doesn't come through prayers,
Peace comes through responsible action.
When the invader stomps on innocent lives,
Not choosing a side is a consent to oppression.
Ask us for water, we won't let you go unfed,
But do not mistake our gentleness as fear.
If you so much as lay a finger on our home,
We'll defend it with our blood, sweat 'n tears.
We ain't no coward to selfishly seek security,
When our land is being ransacked by raccoons.
When the lives of our loved ones are at stake,
We'll break but never bend to oligarchical buffoons.
The love of our families is what keeps us breathing.
To preserve their smiles, we shall happily die fighting.

20. Responsibility and Rebellion

When a tyrant invades, prayers do nothing. So, either take up arms against such invasion, or help those on the ground with resources. This is the reason I've never been an advocate of the prehistoric practice of naïve nonviolence, nor have I ever been an advocate of reckless rebellion.

To be civilized human beings, beings who are responsible, beings who are accountable, beings who don't shut their eyes at the sight of inhumanity, we gotta realize that we don't live in an ideal world. We may turn our back at inhumanity, but it doesn't magically end inhumanity.

We may avoid being affected by an inhumanity by walking away from it, but remember this - in a world run by indifference nobody is safe for long. Sooner or later, inhumanity catches up to everybody, unless we take a stand against it today, everyday, whether it is committed on us or on complete strangers.

Walking away is not an option, no matter how safe it feels at the moment. How long will you walk away? How far will you walk away? I do recognize that in rare occasions retreat may be the only way, but the problem is that, we have made retreat our habit, without the tiniest spark of will to stand up to inhumanity, regardless of whether it is committed on us or others.

When inhumanity is committed on others, we turn our back, when it's committed on us, we compromise. That's how the world works, nay, that's how we work - we the so-called civilized beings.

What civilized!

What sentient!

What sapient!

We haven't even developed the spine to stand up to oppression and dehumanization!

Then how on earth could we call ourselves civilized, sentient, and sapient!

Just because we have atom bomb, doesn't mean we have an atomic heart – not yet anyway.

21. What is An Advanced Species

Sending a couple of probes into space doesn't make us an advanced species. When we start to feel responsible for the welfare of our fellow human beings, only then we shall become truly advanced, no matter our capacities of science and technology.

Remember, humanity without science is fragile, science without humanity is lethal. When the humans have humanity, everything is alright with the world, but when those very humans are anemic of humanity, no amount of science and technology can save this world, nor can a thousand bibles.

If you wanna rebel, rebel out of responsibility, not recklessness – rebel out of accountability, not impulse. That's where a civilized revolution differs from brainless mob violence. Rebellion is good, it keeps us growing, but don't confuse rebellion with misdemeanor - don't confuse revolution with misdemeanor.

Rebellion just for the sake of rebellion accomplishes nothing. Rebel against tyranny, not against every little regulation that feels a little inconvenient to you. Learn to distinguish between inconvenience and injustice. The problem is, in today's world most people consider revolution as inconvenient, and regulation as injustice. So they get their frustrations out on the innocent janitor, and keep quiet in front of the corrupt bureaucrat.

22. Our Mess Our Marvel

All are so obsessed with comfort and luxury, that they rebel most vehemently when their wi-fi is down, but do nothing when their neighbor is down, when a fellow human being is down.

In short, they rebel more for comfort and luxury than for justice and equality, than for human welfare. This must change. If we are to lay the foundation of a civilized world, this pathetic habit of ours must change. This primitive narrowmindedness of ours must change.

And we are not going to change that by retaliating hate with hate, we are going to change that by overwhelming all hate with our sense of love, community and accountability. Remember, courage of the savage is in their weapon, courage of the reformer is in their conviction.

Now the question is, is your conviction of humanity stronger than your biological inclination for inhumanity! If it is, then no external inhumanity stands a chance against the glaring beacon of humanness that you are. Let's take the atrocities faced by our sisters and brothers in Ukraine, for example.

The only people who can end Putin's reign of terror for good, are not the governments of the world, but the citizens of the world. Sisters and brothers of planet earth, if you stay silent now, the blood of countless innocents will be on your hands. Awake, arise, and treat the Putin pandemic, like you treated the Covid pandemic.

No tyrant can continue his tyranny unless the people permit it. When a tyrant wreaks havoc, the question is not, why is he doing it - the question is, what the heck are the people doing! So it all comes down to the people's conviction of humanity - it all comes down to your conviction of humanity.

How far are you willing to go to deter the troubles faced by humanity!

If it's a mess, it's our mess. If it's a marvel, it's our marvel. We gotta decide, whether we'll make a mess or a marvel - whether we'll be the revolution towards a better world, or regress into a bitter world!

Remember, when the law fails to defend people, people have to defend themselves, or to be more accurate, they have to defend each other, they have to look out for one another. When crisis hits any community of the world, it is the human responsibility of all the communities of the world to reach out in assistance.

For example, in the event of a war, even if you are not able to stop a war, there's always something you can do to help those distraught by war. I'll say it to you plainly – a refugee saved is a world saved.

23. Tale of A Heroic Heart

A refugee saved is a world saved. However, it ain't enough! We must at the same time focus on building a world where war becomes a distant memory. And the only way to do that is to take our so-called civic duty as everyday responsibility. I say so-called, because in reality, there is no such thing as civic duty, it's just plain ordinary humanity – it's just plain accountability, that sets a human apart from animals.

And when this accountability is fully active in you, it will eat you alive till you reach out to help those in misery, to help those affected by the atrocities of tyranny. Don't ask permission, just leap out to help. Because, any law that says helping is illegal, automatically illegitimizes itself.

Let me elaborate. Above-the-law tyranny needs above-the-law intervention. Because law that fails to prevent or even deter tyranny defeats the purpose of its existence.

But mark you, exception excepted, assassinating a tyrant is not the solution, it only makes them a martyr to their followers. Stand up to them, strip them of their position, then throw 'em in jail.

There's nothing more torturous to a megalomaniacal tyrant than rotting behind bars like a two-bit criminal.

And this responsibility is to be borne, not by the officers of law, but by the officers of civilization, that is, the civilians. No matter how powerful and resourceful a tyrant is, they are never stronger than a brave and responsible citizenry.

24. Sonnet of Human Duty

Sonnet of Human Duty

To deliver humanity from inhumanity,
Is the duty of every human.
To deliver the innocent from injustice,
Is the duty of every human.
The indifferent may call it god complex,
Apathetic pessimists may call it idealism.
I call it the meaning of life and sanity,
The opposite is just a sign of doofusism.
Differences won't destroy the world,
Indifference is far more ominous.
The problem is not the evil doers,
But the silent spectators.
Mark me well, the day I stay silent is the day,
Lady liberty throws her torch away.

25. Distance Lends no Enchantment

You know what the problem is - people are so obsessed with fictitious superheroes, that they've forgotten all about their real heroic heart.

Some may say, superheroes are inspirational. And I agree that they are to some extent. But despite all that inspiration, if you don't stand up to the inhumanities of your society when it's most needed, what's the point of it all!

Different people find inspiration in different things, that's completely fine, but the point is, inspiration that doesn't come to the aid of humanity in their time of need, is no inspiration to begin with. Remember, it's more important to be a hero, than worship a hero. Just like, it's more important to act as a hero, than be worshipped as a hero.

Be a hero, that is, be a human. You see, every true human is a hero, but the problem is, not all who look human are actually human, in thought, feeling and action. Be human, and get close to people - to help them, to heal them, to listen to them. Don't be afraid - don't be afraid to be hurt. So what if you are hurt - the very thought of bringing joy in the life of another person ought to light up your own heart like the Rockefeller tree on Christmas Eve.

Distance and separation are peddled in this world of ours in many forms. There is this old saying even, that distance lends enchantment. I don't know who said it - I could google, but I am not bothered with that right now. The point is, there is this notion that when we maintain a certain distance from people, we gain respect from them.

But here's the thing. Distance doesn't lend enchantment, it only lends fake enchantment - distance lends delusion, whereas closeness lends real enchantment. We gotta get closer and closer, and closer still, so that our breaths become one, our heartbeats become one, the gush of blood through our veins and the rush of electricity through our nerves become one - one uncorrupted, unbending, timeless force of ascension.

26. Love is An Eternal Torment

Be hurt, fall down, be devastated - you'll survive - a genuine human always survives - it's only the selfish who never truly live and love, in fear of failure and devastation. Come delight, come devastation, the aim of love is to love, with or without reciprocation.

The only thought that torments the mind of a lover 24/7 is the welfare of their loved ones. Love is an eternal torment, but a sweet torment no less. I fell in love with humankind in my early teenage years. Since then I've been devastated at every little crisis inflicted upon people anywhere in the world.

In fact, right now although I am dutybound to continue my work, every second I am dying inside, for Ukraine. I'm dying for Afghanistan, I'm dying for Palestine, I'm dying for Kashmir. Even my pen pours blood. And this bleeding won't stop till I put an end to the bloodshed of the innocents.

Ölüyorum ben, Ukrayna için ölüyorum, Afganistan için ölüyorum, Filistin için ölüyorum, Keşmir için ölüyorum. Kalemim bile kan döküyor. Masumların kanaması durana kadar, bu kanamam durmuyor.

And this doesn't make me some sort of great peace activist - to me, this sense of desperation at the sight of the slightest agony of others is the first sign of individual humanity. In short, this ain't humanitarianism, this ain't activism, this ain't altruism, it's just plain non-ismistic humanness.

To think for others, to feel for others, to act for others, that's humanity. And one who cares for none of it, either out of a sense of intellectual supremacy or out of sheer bigotry, ain't no human to begin with.

27. Love Liberty Bondage
(The Sonnet)

Love Liberty Bondage
(The Sonnet)

Love is liberty, love is bondage,
This won't make sense to an egotist.
Love is liberty when unselfish,
Bondage when selfish.
To be bold yet gentle and unselfish,
That is the whole of love eternal.
Whom you love, you'll die to protect,
To die for love is to be immortal.
Mere reading love stories means nothing,
Become a radical new story of love ever told.
Love is degradation as well as salvation,
When unselfish we rise, when selfish we fall.
A drop of lover's sweat outdivines barrels of holy water.
Only love is divine, rest are lesser echoes from days afar.

28. Mind Over Masquerade

Be a human, live amongst humans - that's the motto for a true human. But mark you, I'm not talking about puritanism, I'm not talking about perfectionism, what I'm talking about is, a human being a human beyond the exterior. I have nothing against the exterior, but when a species puts all its attention on the exterior, it ain't no advanced species, no matter how much we yell as such.

Advance my friend, advance in heart, before you advance in head. Advance in mind, before you advance in masquerade. You see, all of us are taught by our society to masquerade as humans, instead of being actually human.

Pretense, pretense, pretense - it's all about putting up a good pretense.

And it's been going on like this since time immemorial. And every time someone came forward to speak up for genuine humanity above all the traditional masquerade, people made messiahs out of them and used them as fodder for further divisionist pretenses.

It happened to Jesus, it happened to Gautama, it happened to Nanak. I just hope that it doesn't happen to me. I just hope that this time you are aware enough to not fall for all that sectarian worship nonsense.

Christ never said, love thy neighbor only if they accept me as him one true messiah. Buddha never said, help your fellow being only if they accept him as the one true enlightened being. And as for me, you'd know by now that I've always asked you to stay away from all that worship nonsense altogether.

29. Be Possessed

I am not separate from you that you are to worship me, I am just a reflection of you. Just like all the giants of history were reflections of you. If Christ could forget all division, if Buddha could forget all division, if I could forget all division, so can you, and so can every single living human being.

It's only a matter of will. And that will is a question of character. A human character always leans towards nondivision and assimilation, whereas an animal character always leans towards division and discrimination.

Be possessed with nondivision, be possessed with assimilation, no matter how much you are made to believe otherwise by this prehistorically possessed savage world. Be possessed with the truth of unification, and sever the ties to all lesser truths, for any act of division is an abomination of truth, even if it is backed up by all the facts in the world.

To put it another way, possess this world with your oneness, before it possesses you with its selfishness. And believe you me, unless you let lose your spirit of unselfishness, the selfishness of society always succeeds in making yet another materialistic moron out of you.

Society is slave to habit, it is slave to tradition, it has no particular affinity to growth and unification, not yet anyway.

So, what to do?

Simple - be the first person to break out of that slavery. Because, at the end of the day, all slavery is in the mind. Once you wipe out all slavery from your heart, slaveries of the world will fade away alright.

30. No Obligation

You have to become the earthling impossible, only then the people around you will foster the courage and drive to be human themselves. It's not a compulsion, it's not an obligation, it's just plain, ordinary, existential duty. And those who still think, this is kind of an obligation, to them I say - this is no more an obligation than drinking water is.

You are not obligated to drink water, but you can't live without it. Likewise, you are not obligated to help anyone, but a true human can never live without helping someone in need - a true human never gives in to tradition at the expense of their humanity - a true human never peddles nor buys death in the name of heritage while vilifying the value of life.

That is why, long ago, I wiped out my cultural identity, I wiped out my religious identity, I wiped out my national identity as well as my gender identity. In short, I wiped myself out from my psyche, only then I found a place in each and every heart of this world, only then I became the voice of each and every person on earth, no matter their color, culture, gender or profession.

And this is easier than it looks. All you gotta do is rise above all those designations that society has been imposing on you ever since your birth. I am not saying that just because I got rid of all my socially imposed identities, you have to do the same. All I am asking is that even if you choose to keep those identities, never let them overpower your universal humanity.

31. Kindness No Obligation
(The Sonnet)

Kindness No Obligation
(The Sonnet)

Those who feel kindness is an obligation,
Don't really feel but crawl as walking dead.
Those who think society ain't their responsibility,
Don't think, they're just specimens of mental midget.
Giants are those who lay themselves down,
For the welfare of every single soul around.
Intellect is a tool for, not a subject of, greatness and glory,
The root of all greatness is a gentle heart unbound.
Kindness is more than a trait, just like accountability,
These things make a human out of an animal.
Selfishness is more than a flaw, just like egotism,
These things keep an animal from becoming human.
Little selfishness is ok so long as your humanity is in charge.
We've been animal long enough, now let's be giants on guard.

32. Frivolity of Identity

I am a human first, scientist second, and poet last. It's all about priority. I said I am a scientist, but don't make the mistake of thinking of me as yet another shaky scientist. Before I was a scientist, I was a monk - before I was a monk, I was an engineering student – and even before that I was a martial artist. So be very careful, for there's nothing more dangerous than a wounded scientist.

Science is literally the only super power in the world. And I've been playing with science, before I could speak english. When my teenage peers were obsessing over getting high, I was obsessed with building circuits. I gave it all up, because society has plenty innovators, but zero reformer scientist.

So if you want to be a scientist, don't just be a scientist, be a reformer scientist, be a humanitarian scientist. As I said, science is a super power, but without a humanitarian heart to guide it in the right direction, it always ends up doing more harm than good.

It is this simple. Your first and foremost identity is human, all other identities are secondary. And all these secondary identities are meant to nourish and aid the primary identity. Any identity that helps you be more human, is a good identity, whereas any identity that diminishes your humanity must be thrown away at once.

To put it another way, humanity of a human being is much more than mere identity, it is existence. In short, identity later, humanity first. Identity is necessary, identity is imperative, but the problem is, often we get drowned in our identity so deeply that we forget the fundamental fact that we are human above all else. That's when our identity becomes our curse, and not just our curse as individuals, but in fact, the curse of all humankind.

Your identity has far wider implication in society than you can imagine, which means how you see yourself makes a direct impact on how the society sees itself - which means that if there is no place for integration in your identity there's no way there'll be integration in society.

33. Energy and Ethics
(The Sonnet)

Energy and Ethics
(The Sonnet)

One AA battery lights up a house with an LED,
Or it can be used to set fire to it with a spark.
Energy has no ethical polarity, only potential,
Ethics of energy lie in the hands of its wielder.
Society just needs an excuse to escape the blame,
Sometimes they blame science, other times politics.
The real problem is none but the society itself,
Particularly our age-old selfish histrionics.
No society is born human, not yet anyway,
It falls on the original humans to make it human.
Choose science, faith, politics or civil service,
Touch of a human makes medicine even out of poison.
Science doesn't define the scientist, scientist defines the science.
Hence I'm a servant scientist who uses science for deliverance.

34. Coding Sonnet

Coding Sonnet

One of the most powerful tools of science is coding,
A string of illegible characters can make or break a society.
145,000 lines of code landed Armstrong 'n Aldrin on the moon,
And 2 billion of them are working to satisfy everyday curiosity.
But this awesome force is still used mostly to generate revenue,
Welfare of humanity isn't a priority here, but a mere suggestion.
That's why the coding marvel that set out to connect the world,
Has become a playground for conspiracy, bigotry and division.
Learn from the horrific blunders of society's founding coders,
Make humanity the primary command of every code you write.
A code that doesn't lift the society is nothing but a hideous bug,
Zeros and Ones know no good or bad, unless by you it is defined.
Uncle Ben once said, with great power comes great responsibility.
I say to you today, a humane code facilitates a humane society.

35. Equality Begins With You

I repeat, if there is no integration in you, there won't be any integration in the world! If there is no justice in you, there won't be any justice in the world. If there is no sense of equality in you, there won't be any equality in the world.

Let me demonstrate with an example. Why should women have to give up their name upon marriage, as if they are nothing but hood ornaments to their husbands! And why should a child be identified only by their father's name and not the mother's, who by the way, is the root of all creation - who is creation!

I'm not saying that I have all the answers, all I am asking is that you scrutinize these age-old habits that we have brainlessly accepted as the norm. The point is, we are never going to have a civilized society with equity as foundation, unless we acknowledge and abolish such filthy habits that we've been practicing as tradition.

Showing off our skin-deep support for equality few days a year doesn't eliminate all the discriminations from the world, we have to live each day as the walking proof of equality, ascension and assimilation.

So, no more continuing the moronity of our ancestors in the name of tradition, in the name of heritage! No More!

Be a human, a gentalist, be the whole humanity of tomorrow in a person of the present. Remember, there is no greater religion, than religious harmony, there is no greater culture, than cultural integration, there is no greater nationality than inter-national amalgamation.

When you find out that all pursuit of happiness is nonsense, only service is true sense, that's when human life begins - that's when humanity begins.

It's this service that makes a human out of an animal.

It's unselfishness that makes a human out of an animal.

36. One Day Ain't Enough
(The Sonnet)

One Day Ain't Enough
(The Sonnet)

Nature is beautiful when we are beautiful,
Not in body but in mind.
World is beautiful when we are beautiful,
Not in body but in mind.
Society is just when we are just,
Not merely in talk but in action.
World has equity when we exude equity,
Not insta-equity, but one of slow but sure ascension.
It's good to dedicate certain days to certain cause,
Greater still is to dedicate a life to the cause of humanity.
It's okay to shout about rights and dignity on occasion,
Human is one who lives each day for others' rights 'n dignity.
An apathetic society yells about equality on specific days.
An accountable human needs no occasion to roar across dismay.

37. Fabric of Stars
(The Sonnet)

Fabric of Stars
(The Sonnet)

Rise or fall doesn't matter,
If you've helped a few people.
Live or die doesn't matter,
If you've helped a few people.
The point of life is not to live,
Any more than it is to just eat.
The point of life is to lift lives,
In their smile is victory, in tears defeat.
To win over enemies is ridiculously easy,
To win over hearts is the real act of valor.
Muscles wither, clothes get torn to pieces,
Valor and virtue can't be bound by no graveyard.
Graves are for animals and gutter-crawling worms.
Helpers get forever etched upon the fabric of stars.

38. Look At The Stars
(The Sonnet)

Look At The Stars
(The Sonnet)

Look up my friend, look at the stars,
You know some of them exploded long ago.
Yet their light keeps shining even when they're gone,
For none of their rays is tainted by ego.
Not a kernel of kindness ever goes to waste,
Not a gesture of gentleness ever goes awry.
The unselfish one is the happiest person in the world,
You'll find joy when you answer someone's cry.
You're thirsty, you seek a glass of water,
That is just plain necessity.
Someone else is thirsty, you share your last glass,
That my friend, is plain humanity.
When self-preservation turns trivial, 'n humanity common sense,
That's when a star is born, amidst all self-serving nuisance.

39. Reformer is The Remedy

The remedy for all malice in the world is sacrifice. There is no civilized life without sacrifice, there is no world without sacrifice, there is no future without sacrifice, there is no human without sacrifice.

A civilized world begins when sacrifice begins. But sacrifice doesn't mean you demanding the sacrifice of another for your own gain, rather it means to lay down your own life for the welfare of others. That's sacrifice, that's service - that, my friend - is human life. In fact, if you go beyond the words, you'll realize, life and sacrifice are one and the same, life and service are one and the same.

Only service can free the self, not happiness, not intellect, not fame and fortune. So, stand up and serve - serve with all your might, service with all your height, serve with all your sight. Live to serve, serve to live, that's the motto for the braveheart human - nay, that's the motto for the human, period.

The world has a ridiculously short attention span. It cannot stick to any one cause for more than a few days. They forgot about Palestine, they forgot about Afghanistan, they forgot about

Jallianwala Bagh, and they'll soon forget about Ukraine as well. The world forgets, but the suffering of the people continues.

Don't be that world my friend, be a better world, a civilized and responsible world, only then we'll be able to prevent another Palestine crisis, another Afghanistan crisis, another Ukraine crisis, otherwise these events will keep recurring until everybody is six feet under.

BIBLIOGRAPHY

Archer M., (2000), Being Human: The Problem of Agency. Cambridge University Press.

Adolphs R (2003) Cognitive neuroscience of human social behaviour. Nature Rev Neurosci 4: 165–178.

Adolphs R, Tranel D, Damasio AR (2003) Dissociable neural systems for recognizing emotions. Brain Cogn 52: 61–69.

Andresen, Jensine, and Robert Forman, eds. Cognitive Models and Spiritual Maps. Bowling Green, Ohio: Imprint Academic, 2000.

Azari, Nina, Janpeter Nickel, Gilbert Wunderlich, Michael Niedeggen, Harald Hefter, Lutz Tellmann, Hans Herzog, Petra Stoerig, Dieter Birnbacher, and Rudiger Seitz. "Neural Correlates of Religious Experience."

European Journal of Neuroscience 13, no. 8 (2001)

Agar, N. (2004). Liberal eugenics: In defence of human enhancement. London: Blackwell Publishing.

Alteheld, N., Roessler, G., Vobig, M., & Walter, R. (2004). The retina implant new approach to a visual prosthesis. Biomedizinische Technik, 49(4), 99–103.

Antal, A., Nitsche, M. A., Kincses, T. Z., Kruse, W., Hoffmann, K. P., & Paulus, W. (2004a). Facilitation of visuo-motor learning by transcranial direct current stimulation of the motor and extrastriate visual areas in humans. European Journal of Neuroscience, 19(10), 2888–2892.

Bernstein R.J., (1971), Praxis and Action: Contemporary Philosophies of Human Activity. Philadelphia: University of Pennsylvania Press.

Bernstein R.J., (1976), The Restructuring Social and Political Thought.

Bernstein R.J., (1983), Beyond Relativism and Objectivism: Science, Hermeneutics, and Praxis. Philadelphia: University of Pennsylvania Press.

Bernstein R.J., (1986), Philosophical Profiles. Philadelphia: University of Pennsylvania Press.

Bernstein R.J., (1991), New Constellation. Cambridge: MIT Press.

Birkhead, T. R., Johnson, S. D. & Nettleship, D. N. (1985). Extra-pair matings and mate guarding in the common murre Uria aalge. - Anim. Behav. 33, p. 608-619.

Beauregard, Mario, and Vincent Paquette. "Neural Correlates of a Mystical Experience in Carmelite Nuns." Neuroscience Letters 405, no. 3 (2006)

Benson, Herbert. Timeless Healing: The Power and Biology of Belief. New York: Scribner, 1996

Bose, Subhas Chandra. An Indian Pilgrim: An Unfinished Autobiography, Oxford University Press, 1997

Bogen, J.E.(1995a), 'On the neurophysiology of consciousness: Part I. An overview', Consciousness and Cognition, 4.

Bogen, J.E. (1995b), 'On the neurophysiology of consciousness: Part II. Constraining the semantic problem', Consciousness and Cognition, 4.

Bremner, J. D., R. Soufer, et al. (2001). "Gender differences in cognitive and neural correlates of remembrance of emotional words." Psychopharmacol Bull 35 (3).

Brothers, L. (2002). The social brain: A project for integrating primate behavior and neurophysiology in a new domain. In J. T. Cacioppo et al. (Eds.), Foundations in neuroscience. Cambridge, MA: MIT Press.

Buss, D. D. (2003). Evolutionary Psychology: The New Science of Mind, 2nd ed. New York: Allyn & Bacon.

Buss, D. M. (1989). "Conflict between the sexes: Strategic interference and the evocation of anger and upset." J Pers Soc Psychol 56 (5).

Buss, D. M. (1995). "Psychological sex differences. Origins through sexual selection." Am Psychol 50 (3).

Buss, D. M., and D. P. Schmitt (1993). "Sexual strategies theory: An evolutionary perspective on human mating." Psychol Rev 100 (2).

Blakemore SJ, Decety J (2001) From the perception of action to the understanding of intention. Nature Rev Neurosci 2: 561.

Colapietro V., (1988), "Human Agency: The Habits of Our Being." Southern Journal of Philosophy, XXVI, 2, pp. 153-68.

Colapietro V., (1992), "Purpose, Power, and Agency." The Monist, 75, 4 (October) pp. 423-44.

Colapietro V., (2004a), "C. S. Peirce's Reclamation of Teleology." Nature in American Philosophy, ed. Jean De Groot (Washington, D.C.: Catholic University Press of America), pp. 88-108.

Carey DP, Perrett DI, Oram MW (1997) Recognizing, understanding and reproducing actions. In: Jeannerod M, Grafman J (eds) Handbook of neuropsychology. Vol. 11: Action and cognition. Elsevier, Amsterdam.

Carr L, Iacoboni M, Dubeau MC, Mazziotta JC, Lenzi GL (2003) Neural mechanisms of empathy in humans: a relay from neural systems for imitation to limbic areas. Proc Natl Acad Sci USA 100: 5497–5502.

Chomsky Noam, (2017) Requiem for the American Dream

Chomsky Noam, (2016) Who Rules the World?

Chomsky Noam, (2010) How the World Works

Churchland, P.S. (1986), Neurophilosophy (Cambridge, MA: The MIT Press).

Churchland, P.S. & Ramachandran, V.S. (1993), 'Filling in: Why Dennett is wrong', in Dennett and His Critics: Demystifying Mind, ed. B. Dahlbom (Oxford: Blackwell Scientific Press).

Churchland, P.S., Ramachandran, V.S. & Sejnowski, T.J. (1994), 'A critique of pure vision', in Large- scale Neuronal Theories of the Brain, ed. C. Koch & J.L. Davis (Cambridge, MA: The MIT Press).

Coyle EF. Integration of the physiological factors determining endurance performance ability. Exerc Sport Sci Rev. 1995;23:25–63.

Crick, F. (1994), The Astonishing Hypothesis: The Scientific Search for the Soul (New York: Simon and Schuster).

Crick, F. (1996), 'Visual perception: rivalry and consciousness', Nature, 379.

Crick, F. & Koch, C. (1992), 'The problem of consciousness', Scientific American, 267.

Damasio, A (2003a) Looking for Spinoza. Harcourt Inc. Damasio A (2003b) Feeling of emotion and the self. Ann NY Acad Sci 1001: 253–261.

d'Aquili, Eugene. "Senses of Reality in Science and Religion." Zygon 17, no 4 (1982)

d'Aquili, Eugene. "The Biopsychological Determinants of Religious Ritual Behavior." Zygon 10, no. 1 (1975)

d'Aquili, Eugene. "The Myth-Ritual Complex: A Biogenetic Structural Analysis." Zygon 18, no. 3 (1983)

d'Aquili, Eugene, and Andrew Newberg. The Mystical Mind: Probing the Biology of Religious Experience. Minneapolis: Fortress Press, 1999.

Daly DD. 1958. Ictal affect. Am J Psychiatry.

Damasio, A. (1994) Descartes' Error: Emotion, Reason and the Human Brain. New York, Putnams.

Damasio, A. (1999) The Feeling of What Happens: Body, Emotion and the Making of Consciousness. London, Heinemann.

Darwin, C. (1859) On the Origin of Species by Means of Natural Selection. London, Murray.

Darwin, C. (1871) The Descent of Man and Selection in Relation to Sex. London, John Murray.

Darwin, C. (1872) The Expression of the Emotions in Man and Animals. London, John Murray; also published 1965, Chicago, University of Chicago Press.

Dawkins, M.S. (1987) Minding and mattering. In C. Blakemore and S. Greenfield (eds) Mindwaves. Oxford, Blackwell, 151-60.

Dawkins, R. (1976) The Selfish Gene. Oxford, Oxford University Press; a new edition, with additional material, was published in 1989.

Di Pellegrino G, Fadiga L, Fogassi L, Gallese V, Rizzolatti G (1992) Understanding motor events: A neurophysiological study. Exp Brain Res 91: 176–80.

Deikman, A.J. (2000) A functional approach to mysticism. Journal of Consciousness Studies 7(11-12), 75-91.

Delmonte, M.M. (1987) Personality and meditation. In M. West (ed.) The Psychology of Meditation. Oxford, Clarendon Press, 118-32.

Dennett, D.C. (1988) Quining qualia. In A.J. Marcel and E. Bisiach (eds) Consciousness in Contemporary Science. Oxford, Oxford University Press, 42-77.

Dennett, D.C. (1991) Consciousness Explained. Boston, MA, and London, Little, Brown and Co.

Dennett, D.C. (1995a) Darwin's Dangerous Idea. London, Penguin.

Dennett, D.C. (1998b) Brainchildren: Essays on Designing Minds. Cambridge, MA, MIT Press.

Dewhurst, Kenneth, and A. W. Beard. "Sudden Religious Conversions in Temporal Lobe Epilepsy." British Journal of Psychiatry 117 (1970)

Dewhurst K, Beard AW. Sudden religious conversions in temporal lobe epilepsy. 1970 Epilepsy Behav 2003

Devinsky O, Lai G. Spirituality and religion in epilepsy. Epilepsy Behav 2008.

Devinsky, O., Morrell, MJ, Vogt, BA. (1995) 'Contribution of anterior cingulate cortex to behavior', Brain, 118.

E. Horvitz, "One Hundred Year Study on Artificial Intelligence: Reflections and Framing," ed: Stanford University, 2014.

Eckhart Meister, Selected Writings

Egidi R., ed. (1999), "Von Wright and 'Dante's Dream': Stages in a Philosophical Pilgrim's Progress", in

In Search of a New Humanism: the Philosophy of G.H. von Wright, ed. by R. Egidi, Kluwer, Dordrecht.

Fadiga L, Fogassi L, Pavesi G, Rizzolatti G (1995) Motor facilitation during action observation: a magnetic stimulation study. J Neurophysiol 73: 2608–2611.

Fogassi L, Gallese V, Fadiga L, Rizzolatti G (1998) Neurons responding to the sight of goal directed hand/arm actions in the parietal area PF (7b) of the macaque monkey. Soc Neurosci Abs 24:257.5.

Frith U, Frith CD (2003) Development and neurophysiology of mentalizing. Philos Trans R Soc Lond B Biol Sci 358: 459.

Farah, M.J. (1989), 'The neural basis of mental imagery', Trends in Neurosciences, 10.

Finlay BL, Darlington RB (1995) Linked regularities in the development and evolution of mammalian brains. Science 268.

Freud, S. "The Interpretation of Dreams", 1900

Freud, S. "Selected papers on hysteria and other psychoneuroses" Journal of Nervous and Mental Disease 1909.

Freud, S. "The Origin and Development of Psychoanalysis", 1910

Freud, S. "Psychopathology of everyday life", 1914

Freud, S. "Beyond the Pleasure Principle", 1920

Frith, C.D. & Dolan, R.J. (1997), 'Abnormal beliefs: Delusions and memory', Paper presented at the May, 1997, Harvard Conference on Memory and Belief.

Gay, Volney, ed. Neuroscience and Religion. Plymouth, UK: Lexington Books, 2009.

Gazzaniga, M. S. (1985). The social brain. New York: Basic Books.

Gazzaniga, M.S. (1993), 'Brain mechanisms and conscious experience', Ciba Foundation Symposium, 174.

Geschwind N. "Behavioural changes in temporal lobe epilepsy". Psychol Med. 1979.

Gellhorn, E., Kiely, W.F. "Mystical states of consciousness: neurophysiological and clinical aspects." J Nerv Ment Dis. 1972;154:399-405.

Gilbert SL, Dobyns WB, Lahn BT (2005) Genetic links between brain development and brain evolution. Nat Rev Genet 6.

Gray JA. The Psychology of Fear and Stress. 2nd ed. New York, NY: Cambridge University Press; 1988.

Gloor, P. (1992), 'Amygdala and temporal lobe epilepsy', in The Amygdala: Neurobiological Aspects of Emotion, Memory and Mental Dysfunction, ed J.P. Aggleton (New York: Wiley-Liss).

Greenspan, S. I. and S. G. Shanker (2004). The first idea: How symbols, language, and intelligence evolved from our early primate ancestors to modern humans. Cambridge, MA: Da Capo Press.

Grady, D. (1993), 'The vision thing: Mainly in the brain', Discover, June.

Gallagher HL, Frith CD (2003) Functional imaging of 'theory of mind'. Trends Cogn Sci 7: 77.

Gallese V, Fogassi L, Fadiga L, Rizzolatti G (2002) Action representation and the inferior parietal lobule. In: Prinz W, Hommel B (eds) Attention & Performance XIX. Common mechanisms in perception and action. Oxford University Press, Oxford.

Gallese V, Keysers C, Rizzolatti G (2004) A unifying view of the basis of social cognition. Trends Cogn Sci 8: 396–403.

Goldman AI, Sripada CS (2004) Simulationist models of face-based emotion recognition. Cognition 94: 193–213.

Grèzes J, Costes N, Decety J (1998) Top-down effect of strategy on the perception of human biological motion: a PET investigation. Cogn Neuropsychol 15: 553–582.

Grèzes J, Armony JL, Rowe J, Passingham RE (2003) Activations related to "mirror" and "canonical" neurones in the human brain: an fMRI study. Neuroimage 18: 928–937.

Gross CG, Rocha-Miranda CE, Bender DB (1972) Visual properties of neurons in the inferotemporal cortex of the macaque. J Neurophysiol 35: 96–111.

Guevara Che, The Motorcycle Diaries, 1992

Hari R, Forss N, Avikainen S, Kirveskari S, Salenius S, Rizzolatti G (1998) Activation of human primary motor cortex during action observation: a neuromagnetic study. Proc. Natl Acad Sci USA 95: 15061–15065.

Hardy, G. H. (1940). Ramanujan. Cambridge: Cambridge University Press.

Hall, Daniel, Keith Meador, and Harold Koenig. "Measuring Religiousness in Health Research: Review and Critique." Journal of Religion and Health 47, no. 2 (2008)

Harris, Sam, Jonas Kaplan, Ashley Curiel, Susan Bookheimer, Marco Iacoboni, and Mark Cohen. "The Neural Correlates of Religious and

Nonreligious Belief." PLoS One 4, no. 10 (October 1, 2009)

Halgren, E. (1992), 'Emotional neurophysiology of the amygdala within the context of human cognition', in The Amygdala: Neurobiological Aspects of Emotion, Memory and Mental Dysfunction, ed J.P. Aggleton (New York: Wiley-Liss).

Halligan PW, Fink GR, Marshal JC, Vallar G. 2003. Spatial cognition: evidence from visual neglect. Trends Cogn Sci.

Handbook of Emotions, Edited by Michael Lewis, Jeannette M. Haviland-Jones, and Lisa Feldman Barrett, The Guilford Press; 3rd edition (2010).

Hameroff, S.R. and Penrose, R. (1996) Conscious events as orchestrated space-time selections. Journal of Consciousness Studies 3(1), 36-53; also reprinted in J. Shear (ed.) (1997) Explaining Consciousness-The Hard

Problem. Cambridge, MA, MIT Press, 177-95.

Harding, D.E. (1961) On Having no Head: Zen and the Re-Discovery of the Obvious. London, Buddhist Society.

Hardy, A. (1979) The Spiritual Nature of Man: A Study of Contemporary Religious Experience. Oxford, Clarendon Press.

Harre, R. and Gillett, G. (1994) The Discursive Mind. Thousand Oaks, CA, Sage.

Haugeland, J. (ed.) (1997) Mind Design II: Philosophy, Psychology, Artificial Intelligence. Cambridge, MA, MIT Press.

Hauser, M.D. (2000) Wild Minds: What Animals Really Think. New York, Henry Holt and Co.; London, Penguin.

Hebb, D.O. (1949) The Organization of Behavior. New York, Wiley.

Helmholtz, H.L.F. von (1856-67) Treatise on Physiological Optics.

Hess, EH (1975) "The role of pupil size in communication," Scientific American, 233(5), 110–12.

Heyes, C.M. (1998) Theory of mind in nonhuman primates. Behavioral and Brain Sciences 21, 101-48; with commentaries.

Heyes, C.M. and Galef, B.G. (eds) (1996) Social Learning in Animals: The Roots of Culture. San Diego, CA, Academic Press.

Hilgard, E.R. (1986) Divided Consciousness: Multiple Controls in Human Thought and Action. New York, Wiley.

Hilton, E.N., Lundberg, T.R. Transgender Women in the Female Category of Sport: Perspectives on Testosterone Suppression and Performance Advantage. Sports Med 51, 199–214 (2021).

Hitler, Adolf. Mein Kampf, 1925

Hodgson, R. (1891) A case of double consciousness. Proceedings of the Society for Psychical Research 7, 221-58.

Hofstadter, D.R. and Dennett, D.C. (eds) (1981) The Mind's I: Fantasies and Reflections on Self and Soul. London, Penguin.

Holland, J. (ed.) (2001) Ecstasy: The Complete Guide: A Comprehensive Look at the Risks and Benefits of MDMA. Rochester, VT, Park Street Press.

Holmes, D.S. (1987) The influence of meditation versus rest on physiological arousal. In M. West (ed.) The Psychology of Meditation. Oxford, Clarendon Press, 81-103.

Holmstrom, David. 1992, Christian Science Monitor

Holt, J. (1999) Blindsight in debates about qualia. Journal of Consciousness Studies 6(5), 54-71.

Holloway RL (1996) Evolution of the human brain. In: Lock A, Peters CR (eds) Handbook of human symbolic evolution. Oxford University Press, Oxford

Iacoboni M, Woods RP, Brass M, Bekkering H, Mazziotta JC, Rizzolatti G (1999) Cortical mechanisms of human imitation. Science 286: 2526–2528.

Iacoboni M, Koski LM, Brass M, Bekkering H, Woods RP, Dubeau MC, Mazziotta JC, Rizzolatti G (2001) Reafferent copies of imitated actions in the right superior temporal cortex. Proc Natl Acad Sci USA 98: 13995–13999.

Jeannerod M (1988) The neural and behavioural organization of goal-directed movements. Clarendon Press, Oxford.

Johnson-Frey SH, Maloof FR, Newman-Norlund R, Farrer C, Inati S, Grafton ST (2003) Actions or hand-objects interactions? Human inferior frontal cortex and action observation. Neuron 39: 1053–1058.

Jackson, F. (1982) Epiphenomenal qualia. Philosophical Quarterly 32, 127-36.

James, W. (1890) The Principles of Psychology (2 volumes). London, Macmillan.

James, W. (1902) The Varieties of Religious Experience: A Study in Human Nature. New York and London, Longmans, Green and Co.

Jansen, K. (2001) Ketamine: Dreams and Realities. Sarasota, FL, Multidisciplinary Association for Psychedelic Studies.

Jay, M. (ed.) (1999) Artificial Paradises: A Drugs Reader. London, Penguin.

Jaynes, J. (1976) The Origin of Consciousness in the Breakdown of the Bicameral Mind. New York, Houghton Mifflin.

Johnson, M.K. and Raye, C.L. (1981) Reality monitoring. Psychological Review 88, 67-85.

Kadim I, Mahgoub O, Baqir S et al. (2015) Cultured meat from muscle stem cells: a review of challenges and prospects. J Integr Agr 14: 222–233

Kandel, E. R. In Search of Memory: The Emergence of a New Science of Mind, W. W. Norton & Company (2007).

Kandel E. R. Schwartz JH, Jessel TM. Principles of neural sciences. New York; McGraw Hill, 2000.

Kanwisher, N. (2001) Neural events and perceptual awareness. Cognition

79, 89-113; also reprinted inS. Dehaene (ed.) The Cognitive Neuroscience of Consciousness. Cambridge, MA, MIT Press, 89-113.

Karn, K. and Hayhoe, M. (2000) Memory representations guide targeting eye movements in a natural task. Visual Cognition 7, 673-703.

Kennedy, H., & Dehay, C. (1988). Functional implications of the anatomical organization of the callosal projections of visual areas V1 and V2 in the macaque monkey. Behav. Brain Res., 29, 225–236.

Kentridge, R.W. and Heywood, C.A. (1999) The status of blindsight. Journal of Consciousness Studies 6(5), 3-11.

Kihlstrom, J.F. (1996) Perception without awareness of what is perceived, learning without awareness of what is learned. In M. Velmans (ed.) The Science of Consciousness. London, Routledge, 23-46.

Kosslyn, S.M. (1980) Image and Mind. Cambridge, MA, Harvard University Press.

Kosslyn, S.M. (1988) Aspects of a cognitive neuroscience of mental imagery. Science 240, 1621-6.

Kinsbourne, M. (1995), 'The intralaminar thalamic nucleii', Consciousness and Cognition, 4.

Kjaer, Troels, Camilla Bertelsen, Paola Piccini, David Brooks, Jorgen Alving, and Hans Lou. "Increased Dopamine Tone during Meditation- Induced Change of Consciousness." Cognitive Brain Research 13, no. 2 (April 2002)

Kölmel HW. 1985. Complex visual hallucinations in the hemianopic field. J Neurol Neurosurg Psychiatry.

Koenig, Harold. "Research on Religion, Spirituality, and Mental Health: A Review." Canadian Journal of Psychiatry 54, no. 5 (May 2009)

Koenig, Harold, ed. Handbook of Religion and Mental Health. San Diego, CA: Academic Press, 1998

Kraepelin E. Psychiatry: A Textbook for Students and Physicians. New York, NY: Science History Publications; 1990.

Lauglin, Charles, John McManus, and Eugene d'Aquili. Brain, Symbol, and Experience. 2nd ed. New York: Columbia University Press, 1992

Lakoff, G. and M. Johnson (1999). Philosophy in the flesh. Basic Books: New York.

LeDoux, J. E. (1996). The emotional brain. New York: Simon & Schuster.

LeDoux, J.E. (1992), 'Emotion and the amygdala', in The Amygdala: Neurobiological Aspects of Emo- tion, Memory and Mental Dysfunction, ed J.P. Aggleton (New York: Wiley-Liss).

Levin, D.T. and Simons, D.J. (1997) Failure to detect changes to attended objects in motion pictures. Psychonomic Bulletin and Review 4, 501-6.

Levine,J. (1983) Materialism and qualia: the explanatory gap. Pacific Philosophical Quarterly 64, 354-61.

Levine,J. (2001) Purple Haze: The Puzzle of Consciousness. New York, Oxford University Press. Levine, S. (1979) A Gradual Awakening. New York, Doubleday.

Levinson, B.W. (1965) States of awareness during general anaesthesia. British Journal of Anaesthesia 37, 544-6.

Lewicki, P., Czyzewska, M. and Hoffman, H. (1987) Unconscious acquisition of complex procedural knowledge. Journal of Experimental Psychology: Learning, Memory and Cognition 13, 523-30.

Lewicki, P., Hill, T. and Bizot, E. (1988) Acquisition of procedural knowledge about a pattern of stimuli that cannot be articulated. Cognitive Psychology 20, 24-37.

Lewicki, P., Hill, T. and Czyzewska, M. (1992) Nonconscious acquisition of information. American Psychologist 47, 796-801.

Manthey S, Schubotz RI, von Cramon DY (2003). Premotor cortex in observing erroneous action: an fMRI study. Brain Res Cogn Brain Res 15: 296–307.

Mesulam MM, Mufson EJ (1982) Insula of the old world monkey. III: Efferent cortical output and comments on function. J Comp Neurol 212: 38–52.

Naskar, Abhijit. "Homo: A Brief History of Consciousness", 2015

Naskar, Abhijit. "What is Mind?", 2016

Naskar, Abhijit. "Love, God & Neurons: Memoir of A Scientist who found himself by getting lost", 2016

Naskar, Abhijit. "Principia Humanitas", 2017

Naskar, Abhijit. "We Are All Black: A Treatise on Racism", 2017

Naskar, Abhijit. "Either Civilized or Phobic: A Treatise on Homosexuality", 2017

Naskar, Abhijit. "The Bengal Tigress: A Treatise on Gender Equality", 2017

Naskar, Abhijit. "Morality Absolute", 2017

Naskar, Abhijit. "Build Bridges not Walls: In the name of Americana", 2018

Naskar, Abhijit. "Fabric of Humanity", 2018

Naskar, Abhijit. "Citizens of Peace: Beyond the Savagery of Sovereignty", 2019

Naskar, Abhijit. "The Constitution of The United Peoples of Earth", 2019

Naskar, Abhijit. "Neurons Giveth, Neurons Taketh Away | Abhijit Naskar | TEDxIIMRanchi", 2019 https://www.youtube.com/watch?v=BNX-Q0ySm80

Naskar, Abhijit. "Mission Reality", 2019

Naskar, Abhijit. "Operation Justice: To Make A Society That Needs No Law", 2019

Naskar, Abhijit. "Every Generation Needs Caretakers: The Gospel of Patriotism", 2020

Naskar, Abhijit. "Hurricane Humans: Give me accountability, I'll give you peace", 2020

Naskar, Abhijit. "Revolution Indomable", 2020

Naskar, Abhijit. "Servitude is Sanctitude", 2020

Naskar, Abhijit. "Good Scientist: When Science and Service Combine", 2020

Newberg, Andrew, and Jeremy Iversen. "The Neural Basis of the Complex Mental Task of Meditation: Neurotransmitter and Neurochemical Considerations." Medical Hypotheses 61, no. 2 (2003).

Newberg, Andrew. "How God Changes Your Brain: An Introduction to Jewish Neurotheology", CCAR Journal: The Reform Jewish Quarterly, Winter 2016.

Newberg, Andrew, and Stephanie Newberg. "A Neuropsychological Perspective on Spiritual Development." In Handbook of Spiritual Development in Childhood and Adolescence, edited by Eugene

Roehlkepartain, Pamela King, Linda Wagener, and Peter Benson. London: Sage Publications, Inc., 2005

Newberg, Andrew. "The Neurotheology Link An Intersection Between Spirituality and Health", Alternative and Complimentary Therapies, Vol 21 No 1, February 2015.

Newberg, Andrew, Nancy Wintering, Dharma Khalsa, Hannah Roggenkamp, and Mark Waldman. "Meditation Effects on Cognitive Function and Cerebral Blood Flow in Subjects with Memory Loss: A Preliminary Study." Journal of Alzheimer's Disease 20, no. 2 (2010)

Nash, M. (1995), 'Glimpses of the mind', Time.

Nesse RM. Proximate and evolutionary studies of anxiety, stress and depression: synergy at the interface. Neurosci Biobehav Rev. 1999;23:895-903.

Nicolelis, Miguel. (2011) "Beyond Boundaries: The New Neuroscience of Connecting Brains with Machines---and How It Will Change Our Lives", Times Books

O'Hara, K. and Scutt, T. (1996) There is no hard problem of consciousness. Journal of Consciousness Studies 3(4), 290-302, reprinted in J. Shear (ed.) (1997) Explaining Consciousness. Cambridge, MA, MIT Press, 69-82.

O'Regan, J.K. (1992) Solving the "real" mysteries of visual perception: the world as an outside memory. Canadian Journal of Psychology 46, 461-88.

O'Regan, J.K. and Noe, A. (2001) A sensorimotor account of vision and visual consciousness. Behavioral and Brain Sciences 24(5), 883-917.

O'Regan, J.K., Rensink, R.A. and Clark,].]. (1999) Change-blindness as a result of "mudsplashes." Nature 398, 34.

Ornstein, R.E. (1977) The Psychology of Consciousness (2nd edn). New York, Harcourt.

Ornstein, R.E. (1986) The Psychology of Consciousness (3rd edn). New York, Pehguin.

Ornstein, R.E. (1992) The Evolution of Consciousness. New York, Touchstone.

Penfield W, Faulk ME (1955) The insula: further observations on its function. Brain 78: 445– 470.

Penrose, R. (1994), Shadows of the Mind (Oxford: Oxford University Press).

Penrose, R. (1989), The Emperor's New Mind: Concerning Computers, Minds and The Laws of Physics (Oxford: Oxford University Press).

Persinger, "'I would kill in God's name' role of sex, weekly church attendance, report of a religious experience and limbic lability" Perceptual and Motor Skills 1997.

Persinger "Experimental simulation of the God experience" Neurotheology 2003.

Persinger, Corradini, Clement, Keaney, et al "Neurotheology and its convergence with neuroquantology" NeuroQuantology 2010.

Persinger, Koren and St-Pierre "The electromagnetic induction of mystical and altered states within the laboratory" Journal of Consciousness Exploration and Research 2010.

Persinger "Case report: A prototypical spontaneous 'sensed presence' of a sentient being and concomitant electroencephalographic activity in the clinical laboratory" Neurocase 2008.

Persinger and Saroka "Potential production of Hughlings Jackson's "parasitic consciousness" by physiologically-patterned weak transcerebral magnetic fields: QEEG and source localization" Epilepsy & Behavior 28 (2013).

Persinger. "The neuropsychiatry of paranormal experiences". J Neuropsychiatry Clin Neurosci 2001.

Persinger. "Neuropsychological bases of god beliefs", New York: Praeger, 1987

Persinger. "Temporal lobe epileptic signs and correlative behaviors displayed by normal populations", Journal of General Psychology, 1986

Perry BD, Pollard R. Homeostasis, stress, trauma, and adaptation. A neurodevelopmental view of childhood trauma. Child Adolesc Psychiatr Clin N Am. 1998;7:33.

Paré, D. & Llinás, R. (1995), 'Conscious and preconscious processes as seen from the standpoint of sleep-waking cycle neurophysiology', Neuropsychologia, 33.

Phillips ML, Young AW, Senior C, Brammer M, Andrew C, Calder AJ, Bullmore ET, Perrett DI, Rowland D, Williams SC, Gray JA, David AS (1997) A specific neural substrate for perceiving facial expressions of disgust. Nature 389: 495–498.

Phillips ML, Young AW, Scott SK, Calder AJ, Andrew C, Giampietro V, Williams SC, Bullmore ET, Brammer M, Gray JA (1998) Neural responses to facial and vocal expressions of fear and disgust. Proc R Soc Lond B Biol Sci 265: 1809–1817.

Puce A, Perrett D (2003) Electrophysiological and brain imaging of biological motion. Philosoph Trans Royal Soc Lond, Series B, 358: 435–445.

Ramachandran VS. Behavioral and magnetoencephalographic correlates of plasticity in the adult human brain. Proc Natl Acad Sci USA 1993; 90: 10413–20.

Ramachandran VS. Phantom limbs, neglect syndromes, repressed memories, and Freudian psychology. Int Rev Neurobiol 1994; 37: 291–333.

Ramachandran VS. Plasticity and functional recovery in neurology. Clin Med 2005; 5: 368–73.

Ramachandran VS, Hirstein W. The perception of phantom limbs. The D. O. Hebb lecture. Brain 1998; 121: 1603–30.

Ramachandran VS, Rogers-Ramachandran D, Cobb S. Touching the phantom limb. Nature 1995; 377: 489–90.

Ramachandran VS, Rogers-Ramachandran D. Phantom limbs and

neural plasticity. Arch Neurol 2000; 57: 317–20.

Ramachandran VS, Rogers-Ramachandran D. It's all done with mirrors. Sci Am Mind 2007; 18: 16–9.

Ramachandran VS, Rogers-Ramachandran D. Sensations referred to a patient's phantom arm from another subjects intact arm: perceptual correlates of mirror neurons. Med Hypotheses 2008; 70: 1233–4.

Ramachandran VS, Rogers-Ramachandran D, Stewart M. Perceptual correlates of massive cortical reorganization. Science 1992; 258: 1159–60.

Rizzolatti G, Craighero L (2004) The mirror-neuron system. Annu Rev Neurosci 27: 169–192.

Rizzolatti G, Fogassi L, Gallese V (2001) Neurophysiological mechanisms underlying the understanding and imitation of action. Nature Rev Neurosci 2:661–670.

Rock I, Victor J. Vision and touch: an experimentally created conflict between the two senses. Science 1964; 143: 594–6.

Rose´n B, Lundborg G. Training with a mirror in rehabilitation of the hand. Scand J Plast Reconstr Surg Hand Surg 2005; 39: 104–8.

Roberts, TA; Smalley, J; Ahrendt, D (December 2020). "Effect of gender affirming hormones on athletic performance in transwomen and transmen: implications for sporting organisations and legislators". British Journal of Sports Medicine. 55 (11): 577–583

Royet JP, Plailly J, Delon-Martin C, Kareken DA, Segebarth C (2003) fMRI of emotional responses to odors: influence of hedonic valence and judgment, handedness, and gender. Neuroimage 20: 713–728.

Rozin R Haidt J and McCauley CR (2000) Disgust. In: Lewis M, Haviland-Jones JM (eds) Handbook of Emotion. 2nd Edition. Guilford Press, New York, pp 637–653.

Saxe R, Carey S, Kanwisher N (2004) Understanding other minds: linking developmental psychology and functional neuroimaging. Annu Rev Psychol 55: 87–124.

S. J. Russell and P. Norvig, Artificial intelligence: a modern approach (3rd edition): Prentice Hall, 2009.

Singer T, Seymour B, O'Doherty J, Kaube H, Dolan RJ, Frith CD (2004) Empathy for pain involves the affective but not the sensory components of pain. Science 303: 1157–1162.

Smith A (1759) The theory of moral sentiments (ed. 1976). Clarendon Press, Oxford.

Schilling, Vincent. 2017, indian country today

Stein, Stephen K. 2017, The Sea in World History: Exploration, Travel, and Trade

Simonsen R (2015) Eating for the future: veganism and the challenge of in vitro meat. In: Stapleton P, Byers A (Hg). Biopolitics and utopia. Palgrave Macmillan, New York (2015), S 167–190

Tesla N. "My Inventions", 1919

T. R. Society, "Machine learning: the power and promise of computers that learn by example," ed. The Royal Society, 2017.

Tomasello M, Call J (1997) Primate cognition. Oxford University Press, Oxford.